Witchcraft and the Occult

Robert Jackson

A QUINTET BOOK

ISBN: 1–85348–888–7

This book was designed and produced by
Quintet Publishing Limited

Creative Director: Terry Jeavons
Designer: Chris Dymond
Project Editors: Damien Thompson, Caroline Beattie
Editor: Henrietta Wilkinson
Picture Research: Liz Eddison
Jacket Design: Nik Morley

Typeset in Great Britain by
Central Southern Typesetters, Eastbourne

Produced in Australia by Griffin Colour

Published by Selectabook Limited,
Devizes.

Contents

For many people, the word 'voodoo' immediately conjures up a picture of the zombies, the most publicized aspect of this ancient African religion, brought to the island of Haiti by the first batches of slaves during the seventeeth century. Zombies are people whose 'deaths' have been recorded, and whose burials have been witnessed, and who are nonetheless found living months or years later in a state of mindlessness. They are not legend, but fact, as anyone who has made a serious study of voodoo will testify.

Zombies are created by voodoo sorcerers, skilled in the preparation of drugs which induce a state of coma indistinguishable from death. In one famous case, the daughter of a leading French family on the island vanished from her home, only to be found years later in a hovel in a native village, a mindless creature dressed in rags. Nothing could be done to restore her sanity, and she ended her days shut away in a convent.

BELOW
The scars of voodoo and the white man's exploitation are not apparent in this nineteenth-century pastoral engraving of Haiti.

OPPOSITE
Devotees of voodoo who were executed for cannibalism by the French colonial authorities in 1865.

The subject of zombies was treated so seriously by Haiti's old colonial authorities that a special law was drawn up relating to them. Article 246 of the old Penal Code states:

> 'Also to be termed intention to kill, by poisoning, is the use of substances whereby a person is not killed but reduced to a state of lethargy, more or less prolonged, and this without regard to the manner in which the substances were used or what were their later results. If, following the aforesaid state of lethargy the person is buried, then the attempt will be termed murder.'

In spite of much research, no-one – except the *hungans*, the voodoo priests themselves – knows exactly how a person is transformed into one of the living dead. But when there is a reason to fear that a corpse may become a victim, his family can take certain measures to ward off this awful fate. The usual method is to 'kill' the person a second time by shooting or strangling him, or to bury him face down, with a dagger in his hand, so that he may kill any sorcerer who tries to disturb his rest. Sometimes, too, the mouths of the undead are sewn up, as it is believed that a corpse can only be raised if it answers its own name.

Once raised by the mysterious powers of the sorcerer, the zombie hangs in the narrow twilight zone between life and death. It can move, eat, speak, hear what is said to it – but it remains completely unthinking and unaware of its condition, and it has no memory of its former life. The zombie's value is as a source of cheap labour; it can be exploited mercilessly and fed on a few scraps of food every day.

Zombies are recognized by their glassy stare and their slow, lethargic movements. Their voices, too, are flat and nasal, an echo of the voices of the *Guede*, the voodoo religion's spirits of death. Only one restriction is imposed on anyone who owns a zombie; the creature must never be given salt. If a zombie eats salt, it becomes instantly aware of its condition – with disastrous consequences. It becomes possessed with a terrible desire for revenge, killing its master and destroying his property before going in search of its grave.

The zombies are, perhaps, the most dramatic manifestation of the voodoo sorcerer's art. However, voodoo magic does not originate exclusively in Africa; it has been influenced to a great extent by superstitions that originated in France, and which were subsequently 'borrowed' by voodoo.

There can be no doubt that the black magic of voodoo is behind at least a percentage of the mysterious deaths that occur in Haiti every year. As in medieval Europe, spells intended to kill or harm a person in some way are cast with the aid of an effigy or image symbolizing that person, although in Haiti this kind of

witchcraft often takes an unusual form. The sorcerer usually sits in front of a bucket of water, muttering incantations designed to lure the spirit of the person he wishes to kill into the water. As soon as he sees the person's image reflected in the water, he stabs it – and if he has been successful, the water turns red.

Haitian sorcery, however, is a two-edged weapon. The family of someone who has fallen victim to black magic are in honour bound to hit back at the person who originated the spell by similar methods – and they will spare neither time nor expense until they have their revenge. The originator of a spell lives in constant fear that God will not condone his crime and withdraw the protection of the family *loa*, or spirits, leaving the person defenceless against the magic of his opponents.

The voodoo sorcerer normally performs his spells at a lonely crossroads or in a cemetery. The actual casting of death-spells is shrouded in secrecy, but the voodoo magician has several lethal supernatural weapons he can use to achieve his aim. The most terrible practice is called 'the sending of the dead', in which the spirits of the dead are sent to harass some unfortunate person. It almost invariably produces fatal results, with the afflicted person growing steadily thinner and spitting blood – unless he manages to find a more powerful sorcerer who is capable of making the dead spirit release its terrible grip.

Whether an invocation works or not depends on the approval of the dreaded Baron Samedi, the Lord of the Dead. The priest strikes the altar consecrated to the god three times with his knife, crying out the god's name with each blow. He is then possessed by Baron Samedi, who speaks through his mouth and orders whoever is appealing to him for help to bring an offering of fruit to the cemetery at midnight. The client also takes a handful of earth for each of the dead spirits he wishes to send and must sprinkle it on some path frequently trodden by his victim. As soon as the victim walks over this earth, the dead enter his body and he is doomed.

In one respect, the voodoo cult stands out from every other form of occult worship in the world. To practise voodoo successfully one has to be a Christian – and not only a Christian, but a Roman Catholic. The voodoo worshipper who answers the throb of the drums and attends the ancient ritual in some forest clearing every Saturday night firmly believes that he is acting like a good Christian – and would be plunged into the depths of despair if, on the following Sunday morning, he were to be refused Holy Communion at Mass.

This strange paradox is caused by the fusion of African and European beliefs. The average Haitian follows the rites of the Roman Catholic Church devoutly, as he has been brought up to do since infancy, but voodoo provides him with a more alive, physical belief which conveniently fills the gaps left by Christianity.

This explains why the voodoo gods share a common identity with so many Christian saints. St Patrick, for example, doubles as Damballah-wedo, the serpent-god, because legend has it that Patrick expelled all snakes from Ireland; St James the Great is also Ogu-feraille, the warrior-god, while St John the Baptist is Shango, the storm-god, and there are dozens of others. Voodoo has also borrowed heavily from the liturgy of the Church; listening to voodoo ritual is almost, in places, like listening to the Mass.

FACING PAGE
The mist-shrouded and mysterious land of Haiti. Its wooded valleys conceal their age-old secrets of witchcraft to this day.

BELOW
Surrealistic painting of a voodoo initiation ceremony by Rose-Marie Desruisseaux.

It took a long time for the Church to wake up to the fact that Christian religion in Haiti was becoming synonymous with voodoo practice. In fact, the first official attempt by the Church to suppress voodoo was not made until 1896, when the Bishop of Cap Haitien organized a 'league against voodoo'. The campaign was unsuccessful and was quickly forgotten, but in 1941, when Elie Lescot was President, a more determined effort was made to stamp out the ancient religion. The anti-superstition crusade that followed was in reality a form of Inquisition, in which all members of the faithful were required to take an oath never to take part in voodoo ceremonies again.

Not unnaturally, this caused great indignation among the people – particularly in a region known as the Marbial Valley, where two priests, one French and the other Haitian, persecuted voodoo with a ferocious and medieval hatred. With a band of followers, the priests visited every house in their parish, smashing every object that was thought to have an occult significance and cutting down sacred trees – the homes of benevolent *loa*.

The effect was dramatic. Dozens of people became possessed by home-less *loa*, even in the Catholic Church itself, and had to be exorcized on the spot. On one occasion, a group of screaming women were dragged before the priests, accused by neighbours of belonging to the feared 'Sisterhood of the Werewolves'. They too were exorcized. The priests then ordered that all the big crosses in the family burial grounds must be uprooted, since voodoo rituals were held in front of these crosses.

The wooden crosses were piled in a heap and set on fire, and at that moment several people began to twist and turn in a frenzy, screaming that they were possessed by Baron Samedi and the hosts of the dead. No amount of exorcism could drive out the spirits, which mocked the priests and prophesied calamities to come. It came as no surprise to the inhabitants of the valley when, in the following year, the Marbial Valley was hit by the worst drought in living memory.

The battle against the forces of voodoo resulted in a technical victory for the priests and their associates – for a time, at least. Then, in the 1960s, came the anti-Catholic campaigns of the late President François Duvalier, the feared 'Papa Doc', himself an adherent of voodoo. The campaigns were implemented by his secret police, the 'Tonton Macoute', and ended with the Catholic clergy in Haiti being decimated by exile. Voodoo once again had a stranglehold on the people.

In spite of claims made by the clergy and others who have come into direct contact with voodoo, the idea that the old religion – which had its early origins in Madagascar – is based on cruelty and blood sacrifice is largely a myth. The fact that the myth is more

ABOVE

This stylized painting by Camy Rocher depicts a voodoo ritual in progress. The attendants and sorcerer are preparing to sacrifice a goat in order to invoke a tree spirit.

universally accepted than reality is the fault of a few isolated cases which, taken together and quoted in almost every work dealing with the subject, have given voodoo a bad name.

Of these incidents, the most notorious is the so-called Bizoton affair, which took place in 1863. A man called Congo Pelle, whose sister was a voodoo witch, made plans to sacrifice his niece to a voodoo god. The child was kidnapped, strangled, cut up and eaten in a bloody ceremony, and a few days later another little girl suffered the same fate. The criminals were eventually captured, tortured and executed – the damage they had done to voodoo was irreparable.

Nevertheless, there is no denying that voodoo is based to a great extent on fear – and above all fear of the dark, of things unseen. The average Haitian peasant will not venture out alone after dark unless it is absolutely necessary – and it is not ghosts or evil spirits he fears as much an encounter with the 'hairless pigs' or 'Grey Ones', bands of sorcerers who are dedicated to black magic and who are so powerful that they form a kind of voodoo mafia.

The 'Grey Ones' cannot be identified by any badge or mark; they are often well-to-do people, living outwardly normal lives among their neighbours. If they are found out, the consequences can be terrible – for them. One merchant whose secret activities were discovered quite by chance was torn limb from limb by a crowd of enraged neighbours.

The 'Grey Ones' hold their Sabbats (gatherings) on certain nights of the week, which they say belong to them alone. They are summoned to the meeting-place by the sharp rhythm of a small drum, which – although it can be heard at great distances by the sorcerers – is said to be inaudible to the uninitiated.

They wear long red or white robes and a variety of headgear, including the traditional conical hat of the witch. In a winding procession, carrying candles, they go to some lonely crossroads where they hold a ceremony in honour of Maître-Carrefour, the Grand Master of Sorcery, asking him to bless their activities. They then move on to a cemetery, where Baron Samedi is invoked, before lying in wait for some unsuspecting victim, who is not

BELOW

A carnival scene in Haiti in the nineteenth century. Virtually all of these people would have been voodoo adherents.

RIGHT
The Haitian revolution of 23 August 1791 was put down by the French authorities with great brutality and served to strengthen the forces of voodoo.

always killed. If he seems a likely candidate, he is given the choice of joining the sorcerers as a neophyte – or suffering an unspeakable death. Not many refuse the invitation.

Ordinary people may obtain a degree of immunity from sorcerers by having one of their souls – each person has two, according to voodoo tradition – extracted from the body by way of the head. A *hungan* places a lock of hair from his client's head in a bottle, together with nail-clippings and tufts of hair from the various parts of the person's body. A package of food, mostly bread and sweets soaked in white wine, is then clamped on the person's head. A white cockerel is cooked and eaten by the person's family, great care being taken not to break any of the bones. These are gathered up after the meal and buried under the bed of the person under treatment.

The main danger attached to this process is that the bottle containing the person's soul might fall into the hands of an enemy of an evil sorcerer – in which case the person is as good as dead, for not even the most powerful *hungan* can help him to regain mastery of the lost soul.

Belonging to a voodoo cult can mean an enormous financial strain, and yet voodoo fills an important gap in Haitian peasant society. In a country where organized medical services are practically non-existent outside the capital, Port-au-Prince, it is the considerable skill of the *hungan* that sees the peasant through pain and sickness. And apart from that, voodoo is a rich source of entertainment. Many people feel that its continued practice is entirely justified, despite its darker side, by the fact that it has enabled the people of Haiti to carry on African traditions and culture. In fact, if it had not been for voodoo, many ancient African rituals would have been lost forever.

But voodoo as a religion is no longer African, however. It is sheer paganism and black magic, dark legend and fairy-tale – and it belongs to the western world. This, perhaps, is where its true fascination lies.

Thirteen-year-old Isabel Garcia had a strange story to tell. According to her, she was washing her clothes in a stream one day when she was approached by an old woman named Maria de Illara, who had offered her money if she would do some errands for her that afternoon. The girl agreed, and Maria de Illara said that she would call for her.

But the woman had not returned in the afternoon. It was night when she came, when Isabel was in bed with her mother. The girl told how Maria had dragged her out of the bed and over to the window, where some strange ointment had been rubbed under her armpits; the next moment, with Maria's hands firmly on her shoulders, she had flown out of the window and away across the rooftops until finally she came to a hill called Jaizquibel, near the chapel of Santa Barbara.

There were others there, too. It had been obvious, the girl said, that a Sabbat was being held, and went on to describe the meeting.

BELOW
A witches' sabbath. Hand-coloured engraving by Ziarnko, from Pierre l'Ancre's Tableau de l'Inconstance des Mauvais Anges et Demons, *1610 edition.*

The Devil, in the form of a man but with three horns and a tail, was sitting on a golden throne; the girl was presented to him by Maria, and the Devil urged her to renounce Jesus Christ, the Virgin Mary, the Holy Fathers of the Church and her godparents.

The members of the coven had then begun to dance to the accompaniment of drums, fifes and flutes. All the dancers wore masks, but Isabel recognized several of them. She also said that she had seen the Devil having sexual intercourse with women, girls and young men, and he had given her an apple which she had eaten. Two hours later, Maria de Illara had taken her home again. Her mother was still asleep and had not noticed her absence.

Another 13-year-old girl, Maria de Alzueta, also testified that she had been kidnapped and taken to a Sabbat in much the same manner as Isabel. In fact, her story was very nearly identical.

The year was 1611. The place: Fuenterrabia, a town in the heart of the mysterious Basque country on the Spanish side of the Pyrenees. The two girls made their sworn statements in front of the town council, who gave orders for the women mentioned in the girls' accounts to be arrested.

There were four of them, and they promptly denied all the charges. One of them, Inès de Gaxen, had already been tried for witchcraft in France, but had been found not guilty. Soon after the four had denied the charge, however, 69-year-old Maria de Illara asked to make a further statement – and this time she confessed to being a witch. She admitted that she had become a witch 48 years earlier, while in the service of one Joan de Tapia.

Maria confessed that she had bewitched several children, including Isabel Garcia, and that she had had intercourse with the Devil scores of times. After her statement, more children came forward and laid accusations against the four women. Two more subsequently confessed; the sole exception was Inès de Gaxen.

THE BASQUES' LOST HERITAGE

The Basque language, or Euskara, to give it its proper name, is the oldest living tongue in Europe. No one has yet been able to fathom its origin; some scholars believe that it arose in the Caucasus, a traditional haven for wandering peoples and lost languages, while others claim that it is an African language. Romans, barbarians and Saracens all failed to subdue the Basques, who are hardy fighters and are thought to have allied themselves with the Saracen invasion of Spain. In fact, they may have been the 'Sarrasins' who mauled Charlemagne's rearguard at the Pass of Roncesvalles in 778. It is even conceivable that the Basques – and the pagan rituals associated with their traditions – may be Punic in origin, arising from the ruins of the Carthaginian Empire.

All four witches were imprisoned, while the town council sent full details of the affair to Salazar de Frias, an Inquisitor of the Church, who was carrying out investigations into the alleged activities of witches in the mountainous areas of Navarre. Surprisingly, de Frias didn't seem to be interested. He wrote a long letter to the council, giving permission for the witches' belongings to be returned to them – and that was all. The council had no alternative but to release the four women, on condition that they left Fuenterrabia and never returned.

Salazar de Frias's lenient attitude was surprising, because in the previous year he had been a leading figure in a great purge of witches that had taken place at Zugarramurdi, in the north-western region of Navarre. This was one of the leading centres of witchcraft in the Basque country, and Sabbats were held in a place known as the 'Field of the He-Goat' just outside the town. There was a sheer cliff at one end of the field, and in it was a large cave which the satanists used as their temple. A river known as the Stream of Hell ran through this cave, and above it, on a ledge, stood the Devil's throne.

The witches held ordinary ritual meetings every Friday night throughout the year, but Black Mass was celebrated on the night before certain Christian festivals such as Christmas, Easter and Whitsun. The Devil himself was said to officiate on these occasions, assisted by his acolytes, and the Black Mass was said in the Basque language instead of Latin.

Contemporary accounts attribute a great variety of crimes to the Basque witches and the 'Devil', or high priest, who presided

RIGHT

A folk dance in the streets of Bilbao. The origins of these dances, like those of the Basques themselves, are lost in the mists of antiquity.

over their gatherings. Zugarramurdi was not very far from the coast, and the witches were frequently accused of conjuring up the terrible storms that swept the Bay of Biscay, sending many a sailor to his death. They were also accused of producing freak storms to ruin the harvest, but these could be silenced simply by pronouncing the name of Jesus. In the early autumn, when a southerly wind called the Egoa was blowing, the witches were also said to use poisonous powders to ruin the crops. Even today, the Egoa is known as the *Sorguin Aizia*, or 'Wind of the Witches'.

The Zugarramurdi witch trial ended on 8 November, 1610, and the witches heard their sentences, which were characteristically harsh. Eighteen repented and were reinstated in the Church, but seven others were burned at the stake, as were the effigies of five more who had died under torture.

A seventeenth-century historian who recorded the alleged activities of witches in the Basque country, Frenchman Pierre de Lancre, acted as chief judge in a series of trials in the Labourd

BELOW

The ancient standing stones of Carnac and the surrounding area seem to symbolize the mysterious past of the Basque people.

region of the Pyrenees. He was a harsh judge, but nevertheless he was a talented and intelligent chronicler – and his works contain valuable descriptions of satanic ceremonies.

De Lancre believed that Satan had chosen the Basque region to be the centre of witchcraft in Europe because it stood apart from the political and religious influences of the rest of Europe. Even the language spoken by the people, a language that bore no comparison to any other – and whose origin is still unknown today – helped to increase the isolation. The Basques were turbulent and restless, fond of magic and wild dancing – and were very superstitious into the bargain. Apart from that, the great majority of the menfolk were seafarers, absent from home for lengthy periods – and while they were away the Devil found it an easy matter to sow the seeds of evil among the women.

When de Lancre and his 'witchfinders' arrived in the Basque country from the French side of the frontier, thousands of people fled southwards into Spain to escape the persecution. They were the lucky ones. De Lancre described how, when he arrived in one parish, the local witches asked the Devil for special protection against the bonfires that were being lit all over the country by de Lancre and his men for burning witches. The bonfires, at least, were real enough.

During his investigations, de Lancre was scandalized by the number of priests who confessed to being implicated in satanic activities. One old priest – so old, in fact, that he probably didn't know what he was saying – stated that he had worshiped the Devil until 15 or 16 years earlier, when he had decided to abandon satanism and return to the fold of Christianity.

The priest admitted to have taken part in the foul and evil rituals of the Sabbat, and signed three confessions. As de Lancre revealed that he had been tortured, the poor old man would probably have confessed to anything if only it meant that his agony would be at an end. The confession was his death-warrant; he was defrocked and then burnt to death in his own town as 'an example to good Christians'.

After the execution, many priests joined the ranks of those who were already on the run from de Lancre's witch-hunting activities. Nevertheless, de Lancre succeeded in catching seven of the leading priests of the Labourd region. Three of these were found guilty of celebrating the Black Mass and were executed. One of the men, an independent chronicler notes, had not celebrated anything for years because he was completely mad – but it seems that neither de Lancre nor his associates noticed this fact. Or if they did, they ignored it.

De Lancre's 'commission' employed the same techniques as witchfinders elsewhere in Europe. Their accusations and trials were based on denunciations made by children, senile people, those who harboured grudges against individuals and suspects who had been tortured until they were insane. The information de Lancre gathered in this way must have been made even more suspect by the fact that he spoke no Basque.

Among de Lancre's accomplices were several quack doctors who claimed to be expert at discovering 'witch-marks' on the bodies of their unfortunate victims. With the assistance of people such as these, de Lancre managed to 'prove' that more than 3,000 people in Labourd had the witch's mark – in other words, an insensitive spot on the body that registered no pain when a needle was plunged into it. Yet although he referred to it frequently, de Lancre was unable to prove that the 'mark of the toad' existed in the alleged witches' eyes, either. Yet this lack of firm evidence did nothing to prevent him from sending his unfortunate victims to the flames, witch-marks or not.

Despite the havoc he wrought, and the innocent people he condemned to death, de Lancre was without doubt one of the most ludicrous witchfinders in Europe. Even the brutal and ignorant Matthew Hopkins, England's Witchfinder General, was

FACING PAGE
This witch-doll, an effigy from the 1700s, was used to harm enemies. Note the scroll, tucked into the jerkin, which contains a written curse.

BELOW
Witchfinders such as England's notorious Matthew Hopkins were commonplace in seventeenth-century Europe. Those of the Basque country were as cruel as any.

ABOVE
Engraving of the paraphernalia used by Henri III of France in his studies of witchcraft and demonology, now in the Tour de Paris, Vincennes. Kings, of course, were immune from the attentions of witchfinders.

motivated by greed; he received a fixed sum for every witch he convicted. De Lancre, on the other hand, had no such motive. He sowed a trail of terror and bloodshed throughout the Basque country because he genuinely believed that every dark shadow concealed a witch.

Whether the Basque country was in fact the hotbed of witchcraft that de Lancre and the others claimed it to be is a matter for conjecture. The fact remains, however, that witchcraft continued to be practised long after the seventeenth-century witch trials, and is still practised in many a Pyreneean village today. Some parts of the Basque country are said to produce more witches than others. Superstition still holds the Basque peasants in fear of witchcraft, and strangers – particularly if they speak Basque fluently – are looked upon with suspicion in many of the more remote areas, for it is believed that a witch can be detected by the manner in which he or she speaks. Another belief is that a person can become a witch simply by possessing something that has belonged to a known sorcerer, or by performing certain acts – such as walking round a church three times. In addition, if a person is touched by a dying witch, the witch's powers are transmitted to that person.

The power of the witch that is most feared in the Basque country is the Evil Eye, and Basque folklore is rich in stories about this belief. One story, dating from the early part of this century, tells how several children living in a street in Fuenterrabia fell sick. An old woman who walked along the street every morning was blamed for putting the Evil Eye on them. The angry mothers of the children caught the old woman and were about to burn her when she was saved in the nick of time by some men who happened to be passing.

According to Basque tradition, the best way to lift a spell is to make a careful inspection of mattresses in the house where the spell is working, since spells are thought to be carried in little tufts of wool taken from the stuffing of a mattress and fashioned into the shapes of animals. If the spell is a relatively unimportant one, a pair of scissors placed on the mattress in the shape of a cross will ward it off; if it is a powerful one, the whole mattress must be burnt to a cinder.

RIGHT
Many witch-jars have been found, containing such things as urine, nail-clippings and other personal objects used in magical enchantments.

The word spread like wildfire. Throughout the whole of the Haute Loire region of southern France, people walked in fear and barred their doors against the sinister evil that stalked the land during the hours of darkness. The body of a young girl had been found on the edge of the Mercoire Forest, a few miles southwest of the town of Langogne. She had been literally torn to pieces. The wolf had struck again . . .

It was said that the creature responsible was a devil, that it was not of this earth. It was as big as a bull, with great steel-like claws

BELOW
The body of a girl had been found by the edge of the forest near Langogne. Something had torn her to pieces . . .

and pointed ears that resembled Satan's horns. It was reddish in colour, with a black stripe down its spine – or so people said. Of course, no-one had actually seen the creature and lived to talk about it – but everyone knew somebody who had.

The wolf's first victim was a 14-year-old girl, whose throat was torn out by the creature on 3 July, 1764. A week later, a second girl was killed. In August, the creature almost completely devoured a 15-year-old boy – and in September, its victims included two girls, a woman and another boy. The killings all took place in a heavily wooded area known as Le Gévaudan – and in each case the victim's heart was eaten.

By the end of September, the inhabitants of Le Gévaudan were in the grip of terror. They had never known anything like it. Wolves attacked sheep and other livestock, but rarely did they molest humans – and then only in the depths of winter, when hunger made them ferocious.

In response to a frantic plea by the town's mayor, 40 dragoons arrived in Langogne. For several days they combed the woods of Le Gévaudan, wihtout sighting the wolf. People began to breathe more easily; perhaps the creature had been driven out of the area.

Then, on the first day of October, a 12-year-old girl was attacked and savagely mutilated near her home in the neighbouring region of Saint-Chély d'Apchier. On 7 October, two more girls were killed, followed by a 20-year-old woman a week later.

The Governor of Languedoc issued orders forbidding women and child ren to work alone in the fields, and organized a large-scale hunt for the creature. During the weeks that followed, soldiers and armed peasants killed several wolves – but the beast was not among them. The despairing people of Le Gévaudan were becoming more and more convinced that the creature was supernatural and, therefore, unstoppable.

Heavy snow began to fall, putting an end to the search. But the snow did not deter the beast. On 15 December, it decapitated a 45-year-old woman in Auvergne. Five days later, a young girl suffered the same fate, and on December 22, the beast was pursued for half an hour by a troop of dragoons – and, according to their report, it literally vanished before their eyes.

Then, on 12 January, 1765, the beast suffered its first defeat. Seven children – five boys and two girls – were guarding a flock of sheep near Villeret d'Apchier. Suddenly, they cried out in terror as they saw a great wolf loping towards them through the long grass.

THE DOG OF DARKNESS

Werewolf legends have been part of European folklore for many centuries, and probably originate in Celtic times, when both wolves and dogs were often associated with evil and disaster. One Welsh legend, for example, tells of Gwyllgi, the Dog of Darkness, a huge animal that stalked the land, paralysing humans with its fearful howl and then destroying them with one glance from its luminous eyes. Norse mythology also tells of a blood-spattered creature called Garmr, which guards the House of the Dead and will do battle with the gods when the Wolves of Hell devour the sun and moon.

ABOVE

Languedoc has always been steeped in the occult. In the Middle Ages the Albigensians, a religious sect who lived in fortresses like this one, were suppressed by a Papal crusade.

ABOVE
This engraving shows the children of Gévaudan gallantly fighting off the beast when it attacked them.

BELOW
The beast was bowled over by a volley of musket fire, but survived and loped off into the forest.

The beast leaped on one of the boys and began to drag him off. The others gave chase, stabbing at the creature with improvised spears made from knives lashed to the ends of staves. The beast dropped its first victim – who was badly torn about the face, but still alive – and seized another boy by the arm. Led by 12-year-old André Portefaix, the others rushed the creature again, trying to stab it in the eyes. One of them thrust his spear between the beast's jaws, forcing it to release its hold. Portefaix cried 'Save him – or die with him!' and stood over the fallen boy, fending off the creature. At last, bleeding from several deep gashes, it turned and fled. (When King Louis XV heard of André Portefaix's bravery, he rewarded the boy by paying for his education out of the royal purse. Later, Portefaix became an artillery officer.)

However, the people's jubilation was short-lived. Before the end of January, as though enraged by its defeat, the beast claimed five more victims. A fortune was put on the creature's head, the king alone promising 6,000 livres to the person who killed it.

On 7 February, 1765, 20,000 men – everyone capable of carrying a weapon – converged on Mont-Grand, where the beast had last been seen. A troop of dragoons flushed the creature out of its hiding-place and drove it towards the Truyère river, where it was to have been trapped by a strong force of peasants. Unfortunately, the peasants went to the wrong place – and the beast swam across the river and vanished in the woods on the other side.

It was sighted again an hour later, and was bowled over by a volley of musket-fire. It scrambled to its feet again and loped off into the forest – but the pursuers were certain that they had dealt it a mortal blow. No creature of flesh and blood could have survived such a blast of musket-balls. But less than 24 hours later, the beast decapitated another girl. And it left no tracks in the snow around the body.

The superstitious people of Languedoc were now completely resigned to the belief that the beast was an instrument of the Devil, and that no mortal man had the power to destroy it. To make matters worse, the Church stepped in and declared that the wolf had been sent by God to punish the peasants for their sins. A dark aura of gloom hung over the whole land. People went about their tasks furtively, in constant fear. And meanwhile, in March, the beast killed eight more people.

On 7 April, after months of fruitless searching, the dragoons rode away from Langogne. As though to celebrate the occasion, the beast tore out the throat of a 17-year-old shepherdess. On 30 April, after claiming three more victims, the beast was shot twice in the flank by a hunter near Saint-Alban. It escaped, leaving a pool of blood behind it – but just a few hours later, it killed a 40-year-old woman.

The beast grew bolder, prowling along village streets after dark and snarling at barred doors. People whispered that it often walked upright on hind legs, like a man, and now a fearful name sped from mouth to mouth – a name that no-one had dared to utter until now. Werewolf!

Then, in May, came fresh hope. For nearly three weeks, there was no new killing. Perhaps the beast was mortal after all; perhaps a musket-ball had found a vital spot. But the hope was soon

ABOVE
The beast grew bolder, prowling along village streets after dark. Now the people believed that it was a werewolf . . .

dashed. In the evening of 19 May, in Servilanges Wood, the beast struck down an elderly woman and devoured her heart. And on Friday, 24 May, the creature made up for its period of inactivity by killing no less than four people in one day. The terror continued throughout June, when the beast claimed several more victims within sight of their homes.

Meanwhile, King Louis was growing increasingly worried in case the peasants' terror flared into open revolt. In July, he placed the Master of the Royal Hunt – Monsieur Antoine – in command of 20 guardsmen and ordered him to rid Gévaudan of the beast, or die in the attempt. The peasants may have been impressed by the colourful uniforms of Antoine and his guards; the beast apparently was not. As dusk was falling on 9 August, it killed a milkmaid under the very windows of the Château de Besset, where Antoine was staying.

A new and sensational rumour swept the countryside. The beast was indeed a werewolf – and it was said that the man who changed into the savage creature had been captured. His name was Jean Chastel, and he lived the life of a hermit in the forest. He had once been a prisoner of the Moors in North Africa; they had tortured him and turned him into a warped, twisted caricature of a human being. Chastel lived in a part of the forest where the beast was known to lurk, and Monsieur Antoine came upon him there one day. The man refused to answer any questions; instead, he gave a scream of fury and launched himself at his questioner. He was seized by the guards and spent the next few weeks in prison.

It was rumoured that while Chastel was in prison, the killings stopped. Whether that was true or not, the fact remained that Chastel was released on 1 September – and the following day, the beast tore a young girl to pieces. On 9 September, the mutilated body of another girl was found, and two days later a mule-driver was attacked and killed. On 13 September, a 12-year-old girl vanished completely; all the searchers found were her bonnet and clogs.

Antoine had hunting-dogs brought from Paris and embarked on a new search for the creature, but although he succeeded in killing a large wolf it was clear to all and sundry that it was not the right one. He packed his bags and left Gévaudan for good during early November, in disgrace.

A month later the beast struck again, attacking two shepherdesses and killing one of them. Another girl was killed on 10 December, and 11 days later the beast devoured an 11-year-old named Agnes Mourgues. There was so little left of her that the parish priest thought it was not worthwhile burying the pitiful remains.

The hunt for the creature continued, led now by a young nobleman, the Marquis d'Apchier. With a force of 90 men, he set out every Sunday morning to search the surrounding forest. But always, the party came back empty-handed.

On 4 March, 1766, at dusk, the beast attacked and killed nine-year-old Jean Bergounioux as he was driving his father's cows home for milking. Ten days later, eight-year-old Marie Bompard suffered the same fate in the wood of Liconesse.

As a desperate last resort, the Marquis ordered his men to slaughter dozens of dogs. The carcasses were poisoned and then scattered throughout the woods – but although many animals died a painful death as a result, the beast was not among them. On 17 April, it devoured a six-year-old girl near Clavières, followed by a 10-year-old boy a few weeks later.

There is no record of any killing between 4 June, 1766 – when a young girl was decapitated – and the end of August that year. It seemed as though the beast was growing weary of its fearsome activities; between September 1766 and March 1767, there was an average of only one killing per month. But in March came a brutal re-awakening. By the end of that bloody month, eight people had been killed – all within the area of just one parish. The next month, the horror was repeated in a different parish.

On 19 June, 1767, a small army advanced into the forest once more, determined to pursue the beast until either they or it dropped. And with them went Antoine Chastel, the father of Jean Chastel, who had fled back into his woods to escape the vengeance of those who claimed that he was half-man by day, and the beast by night.

As he walked deeper into the forest, following the line of beaters, Antoine Chastel cradled his musket in the crook of his arm. The gun was loaded with a very special ball. He had made it himself – out of silver. Reaching a broad clearing, Chastel sat down on a tree-stump and settled down to wait, leafing through the pages of his prayer-book. The noise of the hunt died away and an uncanny silence fell over the woods.

Suddenly, Chastel sensed that he was being watched. Looking up, he felt a thrill of excitement, mingled with fear. At last, the time had come. Standing motionless on the edge of the clearing was the beast.

Slowly and deliberately, Chastel closed his prayer-book and put it in his pocket. Then, sinking to one knee, he raised his musket and took careful aim at the vulnerable spot just behind the creature's left foreleg. The crash of the musket echoed through the trees. When the smoke cleared, the beast was lying on its side, the grass around it spattered with blood.

Cautiously, Chastel walked over and surveyed the creature. It was big – but not much bigger than an ordinary male wolf. The terrifying thing about it was that even in death it exuded cruelty and ferocity. Its long jaws were equipped with 42 razor-sharp teeth, capable of removing a person's head with a single bite. But Chastel was puzzled by the creature's body. It was not really the body of a wolf; the legs were too thick and the breast too wide. Apart from that, the feet were elongated and had an extra claw. The creature's reddish fur was streaked with strange black bands, and there was a white, heart-shaped mark on its breast.

Today, more than 200 years after Antoine Chastel's silver bullet put an end to the creature's life, mystery still shrouds the true nature of the Beast of Gévaudan. Many people believed that the thing shot by Chastel was not the Beast at all – but the fact remains that there were no more killings after 19 June, 1767.

Just how many people were killed by the beast during its three-year rampage will never be known for certain, but the parish records of the area quote at least 75. Added to this, there were 30 cases of serious injury and mutilation.

Some witnesses maintained that the beast was in fact a werewolf – but if it was, it had nothing to do with Antoine Chastel's son, Jean. He turned up safe and sound a few days later, his name completely cleared. The beast may have been a mutation – a freak of nature that combined almost human cunning with an exceptionally strong body. Whatever the truth, old legends die hard in superstitious Languedoc – and the legend of the beast that left its mark in blood across the land is no exception.

The three women stood silently in the dock, never flinching under the prosecutor's impassive gaze. The oldest of the trio was about 70, her eyes radiating malice and hatred. The woman on her right was 30 years younger, and her face was an expressionless mask. Never once, during the entire trial, had she uttered a word. Only the third woman showed any kind of emotion. She was the youngest of the three, not more than 20, and she was visibly bored. Not afraid – just bored. Even though she and her companions had just been found guilty of practising witchcraft and ritual murder . . .

It was like a scene from some dark witch trial of the Middle Ages. But on this occasion the judge was no bloodthirsty witch-finder-general, filled with religious fanaticism and greedy for the bounty he would receive for every witch brought to justice. This was October 1962, the judge was English, and the place was the Tanganyika High Court of Dar-es-Salaam.

LEFT
French painting of a medicine man in Madagascar. Such people still wield enormous power throughout Africa. Madagascar was also the birthplace of voodoo.

ABOVE
The Ngorogoro crater wood, Tanganyika, at dawn. Deep among trees such as these, the black witch Nyamseni committed her abominations.

The trial was the climax of a horror story – a story that had unfolded among the tropical heat and steaming swamps of the Rufiji Delta, where ignorance and fear still held thousands of people in their grip – and enabled monsters like Nyamseni and her evil helpers to rise to power.

Nyamseni was notorious throughout the Delta as a powerful and evil witch. People avoided her sinister, black-robed figure like the plague. In East Africa, witchcraft runs in families; when a witch dies, it is believed that her spirit enters a bottle and stays there until it is reincarnated in another member of her family – who shows that she has been so possessed by twisting and jerking in a fit. She is then initiated into the ancient mysteries by members of the local coven, and takes over the deceased witch's hut and belongings. To refuse to carry on the tradition is to invite a fearful curse. No matter what her circumstances might be, a girl selected to be a witch must abandon her family and friends to enter a world of darkness and fear.

This was the agonizing choice that faced 18-year-old Zabibu, Nyamseni's niece, one day in 1960 when the old witch came to her

and told her that she had been selected for an apprenticeship in black magic At first, Zabibu refused. She had only just married a young man named Masudi, and she did not want to leave him. For several months she held out, although she was terrified in case Nyamseni called down some awful curse on her husband. For as well as demanding Zabibu's services as a student of witchcraft, the old hag was asking another, more terrible favour of the girl. She wanted to use Masudi for what she called witchcraft practices, and Zabibu knew only too well what that meant. Ritual torture – and perhaps an agonizing death.

By this time, Zabibu was half crazed with fear, but still she bravely resisted the old woman's demands. Then, one day in 1961, following a visit by Nyamensi to Zabibu's hut, the girl's husband fell seriously ill. He collapsed with severe chest pains, and fits of coughing racked his body. The local doctors were unable to do anything to help, and Masudi was rushed to hospital in Dar-es-Salaam. There, he made a rapid recovery – but as soon as he came home he fell ill again.

Soon afterwards, Nyamseni visited the hut again and said that she had put a curse on Masudi. He would never be well again – unless Zabibu consented to become a witch. She would no longer have to depend on Masudi for support. She would be free to do as she liked.

It was too much for Zabibu. Paralysed by Nyamseni's hypnotic gaze, she gave her consent. It was the start of a waking nightmare. A week later, Nyamseni brought Zabibu before a meeting of the witches' coven in the forest not far from the girl's home. The hag told the coven's 18 members that Zabibu had agreed to give up her husband to be slaughtered and his body used for the preparation of horrible potions.

The girl's initiation into the realms of horror began in earnest a few days later when Nyamseni took her to an assembly of three covens in another village. Shortly after they arrived, the witches

EVIL SPIRITS

African mythology abounds with the spirits of good and evil. Evil spirits (often harbingers of death), who tend to be more colourful, are constantly striving to hinder the good spirits. Central to African mythology, though, is a rather vague supreme being, the creator of all things, whose name varies from region to region. There is a strong belief throughout Africa in life after death, and the spirits of the dead are a potent force in the practice of magic. One especially unpleasant spirit, Ngworekara, rules over the spirits of the dead. Bad spirits wander in space, their sole desire to torment the living and eat their hearts.

LEFT
Slave traders in Africa, 1796. Such activities undoubtedly played their part in strengthening witchcraft as a means of protection.

moved off into the jungle in a long snake-like procession. Deep among the trees, they halted and formed a circle around something that lay on the ground. Looking closely, Zabibu saw to her horror that it was a young girl. She was stark naked, and although her eyes were wide open in staring horror, she lay quite still. Later, Zabibu learned that her limbs had been paralysed by the effect of a special drug made from herbs.

Three of the witches removed their clothes. As Zabibu watched in fascinated horror, one of them seized the helpless girl's legs and another her arms. A third witch picked up a long, curved knife and severed the girl's head from her body with one swift stroke. Then the arms and legs were cut from the corpse, which was afterwards disembowelled and cut in half. Each of the leading witches present was given a piece of the unfortunate girl's flesh to be dried and ground into powder.

ABOVE

In just such a remote Tanzanian village, Zabibu was forced to poison her newly-wed husband.

One day, a few months later, Nyamseni's assistant – a 40-year-old woman named Zamlata – gave Zabibu a gourd of 'medicine' and told her to dose Masudi's food with it. The treatment went on for several weeks, and the man grew steadily weaker and more lethargic. It was as though he knew exactly what was happening to him – but he no longer had the will to resist. Then came the day when he finally lapsed into a coma. His body was now ready for the ghastly ritual.

Nyamseni arrived with two other witches, and together they carried Masudi away into the forest. Zabibu was ordered to stay behind. In the solitude of her hut, she broke down and wept as the full significance of what she had done dawned on her. After a while, she pulled herself together and left the hut. She had made up her mind about what she had to do. She ran to her father-in-law and gasped out the full story.

It took Zabibu's father-in-law several minutes to make out just what the distraught girl was saying, but as soon as he learned what had happened to his son, he went to the village headman. The latter was a Christian, and for a long time he had been anxious to obtain evidence that would help bring the witches to justice.

When Nyamseni and Zamlata returned to the village, they were at once seized by a dozen stalwart tribesmen and tied hand and foot. The old witch glared malevolently at the headman as he towered over her, and spat in his face when he demanded to know the whereabouts of Masudi. Turning, the headman barked an order to one of his followers and stared grimly at Nyamseni until the man returned – carrying a pot of pepper. The headman told the witch that unless she revealed where Masudi was hidden, he would throw the pepper into her eyes and blind her for the rest of her life.

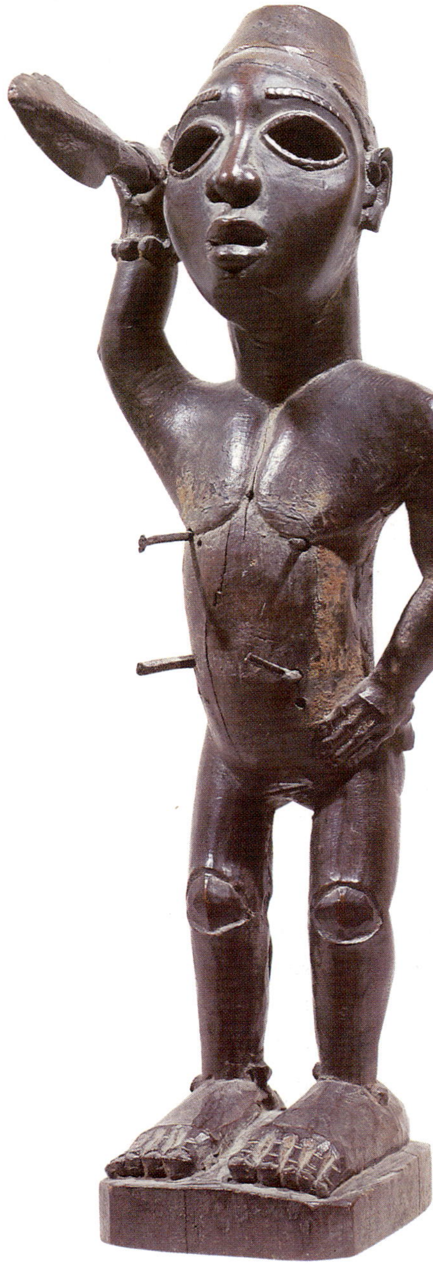

For the first time, a glimmer of fear showed on Nyamseni's arrogant face. After a moment's hesitation, she told the headman all he wanted to know.

Nevertheless, it took a search party of 50 villagers two days and nights before they found the luckless Masudi. He was conscious, but he could neither move nor speak. Later, in Dar-es-Salaam hospital, doctors were completely baffled by his condition. His face, arms and legs were enormously swollen, yet no trace of poison or infection was found in his blood. They did what they could, but it was too late to save Masudi. He died two weeks later, in fearful pain.

It was six months before the witches could be brought to trial. Severe floods swept across the Delta, causing an almost complete breakdown of transport and communications. Finally, the witches appeared before the Utete District Court – only to be remanded to the Tanganyika High Court a week later.

The trial caused a sensation. The courtroom was packed with excited villagers when the charges were read out. Nyamseni, Zamlata and Zabibu were jointly charged with 'making, using, or having in their possession, or representing themselves to possess, an instrument or instruments of witchcraft, and that they also had an intent to cause death, disease or injury to one person, namely Masudi Salum Mwitiko'.

The three were not charged with murder. The doctor's report had not provided conclusive evidence that the kidnapping of Masudi had been directly responsible for his death. As far as the ritual killing of the young girl in the forest was concerned, a full statement accusing Nyamseni had been made by the girl's parents, but had later been unexpectedly withdrawn by them. So had the statements of several other witnesses for the prosecution.

The reason for this was simple. During the six months which had elapsed between Nyamseni's arrest and her trial, her fellow witches had done their work well. The witnesses had been threatened with death, and things worse than death. Even in prison, Nyamseni was still powerful – and black magic continued to have a far greater hold over the people than what was regarded as the white man's law.

Zabibu was the most talkative of the three accused. Quietly, in simple, matter-of-fact tones, she told the court her tale of horror. Then, her statement ended, she seemed to lose all interest in the proceedings. Zamlata, maintaining a stony silence, refused to answer any of the prosecution's questions at all. Nyamseni made only a few surly comments which seemed to confirm what Zabibu had already told.

The three witches seemed to symbolize the power of darkness as, heavily veiled in their black robes, they waited impassively to learn their sentence. When it was passed, the sentence seemed surprisingly light – but it was as much as the law would allow under the circumstances. Nyamseni received six years' hard labour, Zamlata five, and Zabibu three.

The six years were too much for the evil Nyamseni. She died after serving only two. Her assistants were released on time, and returned to their villages. Their fate is not recorded. It is not known whether they were once again accepted into the community, having atoned for their sins – or whether they too met the same fate as their victims, meted out by those whose memories were long.

In the summer of 1942, a small band of RAF pilots – exhausted by heat and dysentery – took off in their Spitfires day after day against overwhelming odds to defend the island of Malta. One of them, a young flying officer, was ambushed and attacked by several Messerschmitts. His Spitfire was badly shot up and he was wounded.

'I knew that I'd had it,' he said. 'I was resigned to the fact that I was going to die. Then something strange happened. I found myself outside the cockpit, looking down at myself – at my own body, still in the Spitfire. I was attached to it by a slender, silvery thread. It was clearly visible. Then, suddenly, I was back in the cockpit again with a jolt that was physical. I pulled myself together and looked around. My attackers had disappeared. I found that I could just about manage to control my crippled aircraft, and a few minutes later I made a successful forced landing.'

The story is by no means unique. Many other people – the victims of road accidents or other mishaps – have experienced a similar phenomenon. Somehow, part of them – call it the soul, or what you will – has left their physical body for a space of time, and then returned to it. Stranger still, there are many documented cases of people projecting their spiritual self across many miles – a phenomenon known as astral projection.

Take the case of one Mary Smith. She had gone to bed early one evening at harvest-time as she had had a particularly hard day on the farm. She had been asleep for about two hours when suddenly

BELOW
The RAF base at Takali, Malta, under heavy German air attack in 1942.

she awoke with a start. Her husband was standing at the foot of the bed, his face and clothing covered in blood. Terrified, she asked him what had happened. He told her not to worry – that he had just had a little accident.

Mrs Smith jumped out of bed to switch on the light, but when she turned round again, her husband had disappeared. Thinking that she had dreamed the whole episode, she went to put out the light. Before doing so, she glanced at the clock on the mantlepiece. It was 10.30 pm. At midnight she woke again. Someone was coming up the stairs. It was her husband. He came and stood at the foot of the bed, and his face and clothing were covered in blood. He spoke exactly the same words as he had done in his wife's 'dream' of an hour and a half earlier.

The two scenes were absolutely identical. Robert added that he had been attacked by two brothers from a neighbouring farm, who bore a long-standing grudge against him. The attack had taken place at exactly 10.30 pm.

This extraordinary story appears in the files of Louisa Rhine, who for half a century studied parapsychology in her husband's laboratory at Duke University in the United States. The story appears under the classification of 'hallucinations', but the word itself does not constitute an explanation. Did Mrs Smith dream? If so, how could she dream, with minute accuracy, future events? Had Robert Smith, during his fight with his assailants, somehow managed to 'project' himself through space to appear simultaneously before his wife?

There are dozens of similar incidents in Louisa Rhine's files. One of them concerns an Ohio housewife whose husband had given her three theatre tickets. She went to see the show with her 12-year-old daughter and a neighbour's little boy. On the way home, they were climbing a flight of steps leading from one street to another, when, on a higher level, the woman suddenly looked up. It was brilliant moonlight, and there at the top of the steps, in shirt sleeves, she saw her husband looking down benignly at them. She never said a word, but the children both saw the man and pointed at him.

'I thought that he must have left the house in great haste,' said the woman, 'because he wasn't wearing suspenders, and for him that was exceptional. When we got to the top of the steps, he wasn't there any more. We all felt a strange sense of alarm, and

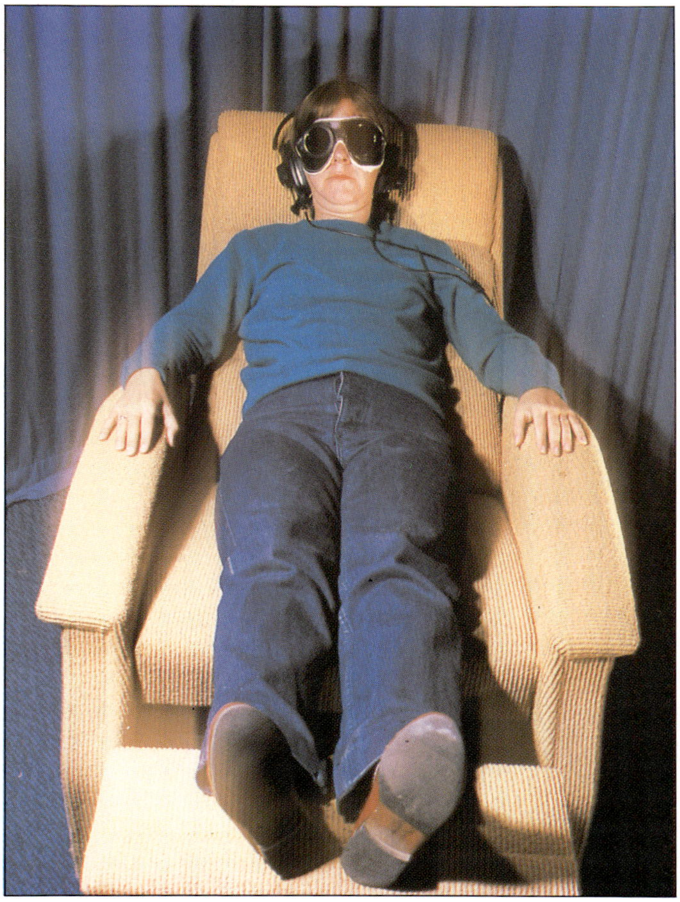

ABOVE

Out-of-body experiments with coloured glasses and auditory induction through earphones being carried out at Freiburg, Germany, in 1982.

ASTRAL PLANES

Astral projection has been practised by the adepts of many occult groups throughout the world for centuries, and there is strong evidence to show that it works, whether intended or not. Subjects who claim to have attained the state of leaving their physical bodies often find it difficult to describe the splendour of the experience, which projects them into a timeless, spaceless zone of pure magnificence. One subject described it thus: 'There is no ground and no sky. No boundaries of any kind. Everything is open. There are other people there and when we want to communicate we can do so without having to listen, without having to speak . . .'

quickened our steps. When we got home, I found my husband asleep in an armchair. He wasn't wearing his suspenders, a fact that struck me at once. But when he awoke, he assured me that he had never left the house for a moment.'

Had she and the children been the victims of an illusion? Hardly. Or had they really seen her husband in the moonlight? While he was asleep, had his spiritual 'double' been taking a quiet stroll around the streets?

At the beginning of 1947, a young American girl named Patricia had stayed in Germany for some time with a friend who was a member of the Forces of Occupation. She then went to England to visit the mother of her friend, whose name was Alan. On Tuesday afternoon, Patricia felt strangely upset and told her hostess that she was worried in case something had happened to Alan. Two days later, she received a letter from the young man, asking whether she had been in Germany recently and what clothes she had been wearing on Tuesday afternoon. She replied, mystified, and from his next letter she learned the facts.

On that Tuesday afternoon, Alan and two other soldiers had been detailed to escort a prisoner to a detention centre 15 miles from their camp. Most of the road was through wooded country, and suddenly they had seen a girl come out of the trees ahead and signal their jeep to stop. They did, and at that precise moment a car turned out of a side-road and sped off at high speed. If they had not stopped, there would have been a serious collision.

The girl who came out of the trees was Pat. Alan recognized her, and so did his companions, who had both met her. They searched for her in vain among the trees, but she had vanished. Somehow, by subconsciously projecting her spiritual body over hundreds of miles, she had managed to appear to her friends in a moment of danger.

For centuries, the mystics of the East have professed mastery over levitation, telepathy, the art of seeing into the future and astral projection. Today, we of the West are gradually coming to admit that the laws of time and space can be overcome by certain individuals, either consciously or unconsciously, and scientists the world over are preoccupied in solving the mystery.

The threads of evidence are scanty, but when gathered together they form an irrefutable picture. One thing is certain: there are people who seem to be able to 'leave their bodies' and project their 'doubles' at will through space, to appear many miles away. Sometimes they have a vague feeling that something out of the ordinary has happened, as in the case of Patricia. In this instance, she was completely unable to control the astral projection.

However, there exist those who can project themselves consciously, as in the following case.

The Italian Army had suffered a severe defeat at Caporetto. It was November, 1917. The Italian commander, General Cadorna, his troops routed, had retired to his tent and was contemplating suicide. Suddenly, a young monk came in and said:

'Come, General, you must not dream of doing such a thing!' Then he disappeared.

After the war, General Cadorna heard of Father Pio, a priest who bore the stigmata on his flesh – the marks of the nails in Christ's hands and feet. He travelled to southern Italy, to San Giovanni Rotondo, to meet the priest. To his stupefaction, General Cadorna recognized the man who had appeared to him in his hour of distress. The holy man recognized him too, and said:

'You came through it very well, my son.'

Although Father Pio several times demonstrated his power of appearing in two places at the same time, he was never able to explain it – nor indeed did he attempt to do so, mainly because the Church placed a ban of silence on those of its followers who apparently possessed occult powers. That Father Pio had the power of projecting himself at will there can be no doubt, for there have been many witnesses to it.

One such was Monsignor Damiani, Bishop of Salto in Uruguay, who made several trips to Italy to see Father Pio. The Monsignor expressed the wish that he might die at San Giovanni, so that Father Pio could perform the last rites for him. 'No', the priest told him, 'you will die in Uruguay. But I shall be beside you.'

In 1942, the Archbishop of Montevideo was awakened during the night by a messenger who told him that Monsignor Damiani was dying. The Archbishop left at once, but it was too late. On a table near Monsignor Damiani's death-bed, he found a scrap of paper. On it were three simple words, written in the dying man's hand. 'Father Pio came.'

A few years later, in 1949, the Archbishop himself made a pilgrimage to San Giovanni. When he saw Father Pio, he was filled with wonder. For Father Pio was the mysterious messenger who had come to him that night in 1942, with the news that Monsignor Damiani lay dying.

It is quite possible that Father Pio might have been able to enlighten the scientists who were interested in his case, but he would never reveal his secret. Until the day he died, he claimed that his sole mission on earth was to bring help and comfort to those who needed it, and it was to that end alone that he used his miraculous powers. Some scientists, who had made intensive studies of Eastern mysticism, were of the opinion that Father Pio must have reached a high degree of mastery in the technique of meditation, on a parallel with the great Yogis of India. Through his faith, he had acquired supernatural powers.

Before she married Sir John le Poer, Lady Alice Kyteler had had three previous husbands. They all had one thing in common. They all died young – and they all died mysteriously.

Lady Alice lived in Kilkenny, Ireland, during the early part of the fourteenth century. She and her family were not popular in the area, partly because they were very wealthy and partly because of their cruelty towards the serfs who were bound to them.

Two of Lady Alice's husbands had been widowers with children, and it was these step-children who were to be responsible for her eventual downfall. The trouble began in 1324, when Sir John le Poer began to suffer from a strange illness – a wasting disease that caused his hair to come out in great tufts and the nails to drop from his toes and fingers. Seeing what was happening to him, Lady Alice's stepchildren began to whisper that it was a mysterious illness just like this that had killed their fathers.

There were other whispers, too – rumours that Lady Alice practised witchcraft – whispers which finally reached Sir John. He demanded the keys to his wife's room, but when she refused to

BELOW
The landscape of Kilkenny, Ireland. Witchcraft began to flourish here in the fourteenth century.

LEFT
Inside Kilkenny Castle, the scene of much magic, intrigue – and perhaps murder.

BELOW
Pope John XXII ordered the formation of what was perhaps to become a greater evil than witchcraft itself – the Inquisition.

give them to him, he took them from her by force. Unlocking the door, he discovered a number of chests that contained phials of evil-smelling liquids and what looked like powdered bones.

For Sir John, the discovery was proof enough that his wife was dabbling in the Black Art. He sent the phials to the Bishop of Ossary – an English Franciscan named Richard de Ledrede – together with a letter written by Lady Alice's stepchildren, accusing her of consorting with the Devil.

The Bishop of Ossary had recently been consecrated by Pope John XXII, who six years earlier had issued the first Papal Bull dealing with sorcery. He had even ordered an enquiry into certain members of his own court, who had been accused of practising magic. This involved charges of raising the dead, causing pain and death by means of images and effigies, and conjuring up demons with the aid of mirrors.

The Pope believed that evil spirits could be imprisoned in rings or mirrors for the purpose of obtaining information about events in either the past or future. To stamp out these practices, he ordered the formation of what was ultimately to become a far greater evil – the Inquisition.

The Bishop of Ossary, eager to please the Pope, duly had Lady Alice arrested, together with 11 others. These were her son by her first marriage, William Outlawe; Robert of Bristol; Alice Faber; John, Helen and Sysoh Galrussyn; William Payne de Boly; Eva de Brounestoun; Annota Lange; Petronella de Meath, Alice's maid; and Petronella's daughter Sarah.

RIGHT
In medieval times it was believed that a woman who spent too much time making herself pretty in front of the mirror would be visited by the Devil and her face would become uglier than Satan's backside.

There were seven formidable charges against them in the Bishop's indictment. First, it was alleged that in the performance of witchcraft they had totally denied the faith of Christ and cast aside the guidance of the Church for long periods, depending on the duration of whatever spells they were weaving. Second it was alleged that they had invoked demons by the sacrifice of living animals, which had been torn apart and the pieces scattered at a crossroads, consecrated by a demon who had told the sorcerers his name was Robert Artisson. And thirdly, Lady Alice and her coven were charged with seeking advice from demons, the premises of the Church being used for this purpose. The charges also included the boilng of a 'noisome brew' in the skull of a beheaded robber; the ingredients included the intestines of cocks, foul worms, nails from corpses, hairs and the brains of boy-children who had died unbaptized – and herbs to add flavour to it all.

From the brew, Lady Alice was said to have made potions that could cause love or hate, or be used for 'harming the bodies of faithful Christians'. On top of it all, there was the allegation that she had disposed of three husbands, and was in the process of getting rid of the fourth when she was found out; that she 'had so infatuated and charmed them that they had given all their property to her and her son and heirs; in so much that her present husband, Sir John le Poer, was reduced to a most miserable state of body by her poisons, ointments and other magical operations; but being warned by her maidservant, he had forcibly taken from his wife the keys of her boxes. Therein was found a wafer of sacra-

RICH WITCHES

In the Middle Ages in Britain, common folk made little secret of their involvement with witchcraft and suffered because of it, yielding much loot to the Church in the process. Then the Church went in pursuit of more lucrative game, such as Lady Alice Kyteler. She was not alone; Lady Glamis, an ancestor of Queen Elizabeth II, was burned alive as a witch in 1537. The Duchess of Gloucester was condemned as a witch and thrown into the dreaded Bishop's Prison in Peel Castle on the Isle of Man, where she languished in dreadful conditions until her death 16 years later. Her companion Margery, known as the Witch of Eye, was burned at the stake, and another accomplice, Roger Witche, was taken from the Tower of London to Tyburn, where he was hanged, beheaded and quartered.

mental bread, having the Devil's name stamped thereupon instead of Jesus Christ; and moreover, a pipe of ointment with which she greased a staff and ambled and galloped through thick and thin, when and in what manner she wished.'

The indictment also stated that sexual intercourse had taken place between Lady Alice and her familiar, the demon known as Robert Artisson, who sometimes appeared in human shape accompanied by two tall companions with 'dark visages' and sometimes as a cat or shaggy dog. Sacrifice was regularly made to the demon in various ways; in one of them, the eyes of nine peacocks and nine red cocks were placed on a stone bridge at a crossroads. Ointment was then rubbed on a long beam of wood; mounting the beam, Lady Alice and her companions could be carried magically to wherever they desired.

She was also alleged to have 'attracted money to the house of her son, William Outlawe, by taking a broom and sweeping the streets of Kilkenny in the afternoon, raking all the filth towards the door of her son William Outlawe and murmuring secretly these words: "To the house of William, my son, hie all the wealth of Kilkenny town."'

This allegation actually appears in a much later account of the trial, and – since it is extremely hard to visualize a woman of Lady Alice's calibre sweeping the streets in front of a crowd of interested onlookers, muttering to herself into the bargain – it is very probably a fabrication.

Although technically under arrest as far as the Church was concerned, Lady Alice and her accomplices were not imprisoned because in British courts, up to this time, sorcery had not been regarded as a crime that came under the jurisdiction of the Church. The only man with the necessary authority to bring the accused to trial was the Lord Chancellor of Ireland, Roger Outlawe – and he was related to Alice's first husband. He decided to take no action, and tried to persuade the Bishop to drop the charges.

The Bishop refused, and convened an ecclesiastical court at which Lady Alice was excommunicated in her absence. Two days after the court had pronounced its sentence, the Bishop received an important visitor in the shape of Arnald le Poer, the Seneschal (or Steward) of Kilkenny and John le Poer's nephew. The Seneschal made it plain that he did not condone the court or agree with its sentence – at that time, when the Church was virtually the supreme power, excommunication was literally a fate worse than death – and begged the Bishop to reduce the sentence. It was no use. The Seneschal left the Bishopric in a towering rage, shouting threats and swearing that he would have vengeance against the Bishop.

It was not long in coming. The next morning, the Bishop set out with a small retinue to visit various parts of his diocese. On the way, they were surrounded by a strong force of men-at-arms led by Stephen le Poer, the Seneschal's brother. With drawn swords, they escorted the Bishop as a prisoner to Kilkenny castle.

The Bishop's immediate reaction was to place the entire diocese under a religious interdict, which meant that every inhabitant

BELOW

Judgement against convicted witches was summary and brutal. Here, an unfortunate is being dragged away to be burned.

BELOW
Frans Francken's magnificent painting of a witches' sabbath, in the Victoria and Albert Museum, London.

The twin villages of Mora and Elfdale lay in the heart of some of the most beautiful country in the world: the mountains and lakes of central Sweden. There was peace here, as well as beauty. The villagers, nurtured by the crisp air that brought a sweet tang of pines with it as it swept down from the mist-covered slopes above the lakes, were robust and carefree. Simple people, few of them were deeply religious in an orthodox manner; yet in their own way, because of the peace and beauty that was their heritage, they were close to the heart of God.

But that was before the Devil kidnapped their children.

It happened quite suddenly. A child grew pale and listless. That night, when he fell asleep, his terrified parents thought that he was dead. His body was unnaturally cold and rigid. In fact, the child was in what would nowadays be called a cataleptic trance. As he emerged from it, he began to moan and thrash about as though in a paroxysm of terror. When he awoke, he was a different person. His eyes had a faraway, ecstatic look; it was as if he were in the middle of a waking dream. A degree of normality returned as the day wore on – but as soon as darkness fell the child lapsed into his uncanny trance once more.

LEFT
The village church of Mora. The local community was deeply religious in a simple way.

First one child, then 10, 20, 50 even 100 were affected in a similar way. A strange, terrifying rumour began to circulate. The children, it was whispered, were being abducted by witches and forced to take part in satanic ceremonies, after which they were allowed to go home again. It was said that the pastor of Elfdale had written a letter to his bishop in which he claimed to have conclusive proof that an eight-year-old girl had been initiated into a witches' coven by a 17-year-old servant girl. An old crone of 70 had also confessed to abducting children and using the innocent bodies for all manner of vile perversions.

Thoroughly alarmed, several of the leading citizens of Mora and Elfdale drafted a petition to the King of Sweden, Charles XI. At that time – it was 1668 – the monarch himself was only 14 years old, and his decisions were made for him by his State Council. The Council – mindful of the fact that the rest of Europe was in the grip of witchcraft fever and anxious to avoid similar scandals in Sweden – decided that the villagers' petition merited an investigation. They appointed two commissioners, gave them the power to interrogate witnesses and to take whatever action might be necessary to put an end to any mischief, and sent them to Elfdale to find out exactly what was going on.

BELOW
Dark and brooding lakeland in southern Sweden. Most Satanic rites were held by water.

It was the start of one of history's strangest and most sinister witch trials, a trial that led to the persecution of innocent children while the real culprits, whoever they were, went free.

The chief witnesses were the parents of the 100 children who were said to have been carried away by the witches. But it was the children themselves who provided the sensational details of the horror they had experienced. In small, stupefied voices, they told how they had been carried away to a place called Blakolla, although they had no idea where this was. There, they had taken part in mysterious rites and orgies, culminating in a feast presided over by a devil whom they called Locyta.

A deathly silence fell over the assembly – 3,000 strong – as the commissioners asked the children to tell exactly how they had reached this mysterious place called Blakolla. The tale they told was incredible, and all the more horrifying for the fact that each child told it in perfect detail, their faces expressionless masks, as though they were reciting a well-known nursery rhyme.

The children said that first of all they had gone to a gravel-pit that lay near a crossroads. There, they had draped cloths over their heads and danced around blindly until they were almost exhausted. The dance over, they then ran to the crossroads, where they formed a circle. Three times – softly at first, then louder, then very loud – they cried the ritual summons:

'Antecessor, come and carry us to Blakolla!'

Then, they said, the 'devil' used to appear. They described him as a big man, with a bushy red beard, who wore colourful red or blue clothes. They told the shocked assembly that the man had been kindly – not at all like the foul fiend the Devil was supposed to be – and that he had laughed a lot. The children had not been in the least afraid of him.

The devil provided them with strange, unearthly animals for the ride to Blakolla. He also gave them witches' ointment, which had the power to make them fly through the air on broomsticks.

The Black Sabbat was held in a big house that stood alone in a meadow. There, the children were made to swear allegiance to Satan. They had to devote themselves to him, body and soul, and were given satanic names. They were also threatened that if they revealed any of the cult's secrets, they would be slowly tortured and beaten to death.

At their initiation ceremony, which was held by the side of a lake, each child was given a bag filled with metal filings taken from a church bell. The bag was then thrown into the water, with the words: 'As these filings from the bell can never return to the bell, so may my soul never return to heaven.'

After the ceremony, the initiates sat down to a feast, the favourites sitting next to the 'devil'. Sometimes the food was excellent; sometimes it was nauseating, a concoction of foul ingredients which the children were forced to eat.

Then there was dancing. While the 'devil' played a harp, the children were made to dance half naked in front of him. Sometimes, they were beaten by the coven's 'priests' out of sheer sadism, and sexual perversions were also practised. In fact, the whole conduct of the coven was closely parallel to that of covens in England and elsewhere in Europe.

The children were also taught how to cast harmful spells. They confessed that on one occasion they had put a spell on the pastor of Elfdale by hammering a nail into the head of a wooden effigy; the pastor confirmed that he had been experiencing unusually severe headaches for the first time in his life.

That was the chidren's story. Fantastic though it appeared to the commissioners, one fact above all others made it seem credible – each child told a tale that was identical, down to the most minute detail, with that of his fellows. Seventy adults were also

WELCOME TO HELL

The spirits of the Norse lands are grim creations, and become more so the farther north one travels. In Finland, only certain evil spirits can pass the Loathsome River and Surma, the guardian monster that lurks on the opposite bank, to reach Tuonela, the Land of the Dead. This is ruled by Tuoni and his wife Tuonetar, who are helped by their daughters Kipu-Tytto, the spirit of sickness, and Loviatar, the spirit of all evil, with her plague-ravaged face and nine children who bear the names of the diseases that were the scourge of medieval times. Tuonetar welcomes newcomers to hell with a mug of ale filled with frogs and worms.

accused of being implicated in some way with the satanic rituals; 23 of them confessed to the crime of witchcraft and were subsequently beheaded, their bodies afterwards being burned.

One thing above all puzzled the interrogators. Although the children swore that they had actually been present in the flesh at the Sabbat, many of their parents were adamant that the young ones had never left the house. Then one of the accused – a girl – admitted that there had been occasions when the devil had only taken away her spirit, leaving her body behind. Still utterly perplexed, the commissioners accepted the statement. They had all the evidence they wanted; most of the accused had confessed, and all that remained for them to do now was to pass sentence.

It was a harsh one. Fifteen of the children, between the ages of nine and 16, were executed. Sixty more were sentenced to be birched, and to be caned severely once a week for a year. No

ABOVE

Harsh sentences were meted out to suspected witches. This sixteenth-century woodcut shows a woman seized by an evil beast and a man about to be crushed by heavy cartwheels.

attempt was made to locate Blakolla, or to trace the mysterious high priest known as Locyta – the 'devil' of the children's story. To the superstitious people, the story alone was proof enough that the children had been in the hands of supernatural forces. There was little point in searching for a phantom.

It was a pity, for if Locyta and the place where the Sabbat was held had been identified, some interesting facts might have been unearthed. And there can be little doubt that Locyta would have proved just as vulnerable as the innocent children he had led astray, and who had shed their blood because of him.

Today, experts who have studied the strange case of the 'bewitched' children of Elfdale and Mora believe that the children were the victims of either mass hypnosis or some form of drug – perhaps a primitive version of LSD, manufactured from certain fungi. Many of the experiences they claimed to have undergone – such as flying through the air – could in fact have been pure hallucination. But there was one major snag: no two hallucinations would have been alike, and the children's accounts were absolutely identical in every respect.

During the trial, the interrogators had completely overlooked one aspect that linked the whole affair closely with the accepted pattern of European witchcraft: the phenomenon known as the 'dreaming soul'. Many witches in their confessions, had admitted that they sometimes confused dreams with reality. One writer, Sinistrari, said in his *Demoniality*, published in 1700:

> 'There is no question that sometimes young women, deceived by the Demon, imagine that they are actually taking part in the Sabbats of witches, and all this is merest fantasy. But this is not always the case; on the contrary, it more often happens that witches are bodily present at Sabbats and have an actual carnal and corporeal connection with the Demon.'

Some inquisitors believed that the Devil had no power to transport a witch's body away, and that the Sabbats were held in the spirit while the witch's material body was sleeping. She was said to lie down on her left side and place herself in a trance, whereupon her spirit crept out of her mouth in the form of a bluish vapour.

All this, however, supposes that the witch is already an initiate and has been endowed with mystical powers. The same could not be said of the Swedish children. They were the victims of some overwhelming external force. The question is, what force?

Suppose a small band of people, far advanced on the occult path, led by a black magician possessing immense powers – powers that included the ability to set up some form of telepathic communication with the untroubled mind of a sleeping child. And not just one child, but 100. Subconciously the children receive an order

ABOVE
Seventeenth-century representation of a witches' sabbath, perhaps based on a scene from a play.

to go to a certain place at a certain time. The next day, the children rendezvous at the gravel-pit near the crossroads. The magician appears and leads them to the Sabbat like a kind of satanic pied piper. Afterwards, the children are ordered to forget the place and the way to it; their memory of the journey is hypnotically supplanted by a surrealist dream. And the next night, as the children sleep, they enter a trance-like state as the telepathic command comes to them again.

Fantastic? Maybe. But today, we know that such abominations are at least theoretically possible – and fact is often far, far stranger than fiction.

As to who Locyta really was, that we shall never know, nor what his purpose was; whether it was an attempt to form a 'new order' of satanists, or merely a means of satisfying his own perverted lust, is doomed to remain a mystery. The adults who were brought to trial were mere puppets; they knew as little about the mysterious magician as did the children. Locyta and his acolytes vanished from the face of the earth.

But old legends and superstitions die hard. Even today, more than 300 years later, the memory is still strong in that part of Sweden of the time when the children of two villages were possessed by dark forces.